The Message of Quran for Teens

One Surah at a Time

Faisal Sartaj
&
Aslam Sheik

TANEESHA PUBLISHERS

Title : The Message of Quran for Teens: One Surah at a Time
Author : Faisal Sartaj, Aslam Sheik
Edition : First (February, 2025)
ISBN : 9789348037978

Published by

TANEESHA PUBLISHERS | *A Venture by -* **PRACHI DIGITAL PUBLICATION**

Regd. Add.: 254, Khuriyakhatta No. 10, Bindukhatta,
Lalkuan, Nainital - 262402, Uttarakhand, India
Website : www.taneeshapublishers.in
E-mail : taneeshapublishers@gmail.com
Phone : +91 8454 812712, +91 8057 812712

Printed by :
Manipal Technologies Limited, Bengaluru - 560001, Karnataka

Foreword

The Message of Quran for Teens: One Surah at a Time is a unique guide, created to help you—teenagers—understand the Quran's wisdom in a way that speaks directly to your life. The Quran is not just a book; **it's a profound message from Allah**, meant to guide you through every challenge, joy, and question you face. But let's face it: sometimes, its deep meanings can feel distant or hard to connect with, especially as a young person trying to make sense of the world. That's exactly why we've put together this book.

Each surah in this book has been summarized to bring out its key teachings in a way that's easy to grasp, relatable, and engaging. From **stories of prophets and lessons of faith, to warnings about the consequences of actions,** this book gives you the essence of each surah in just a few words. Through these summaries, we hope to ignite a spark of curiosity in you—a curiosity that will drive you to explore the Quran in its full depth and beauty.

This book is designed to do more than just explain what's in each surah. It challenges you to think, reflect, and act. **It asks you to consider: What is Allah trying to teach me? How can I apply these lessons to my life? What's**

my purpose, and how do I stay on the path that leads to true success?

We've used AI tools to assist in presenting the surahs in a clear and simple way, but we know no effort is without imperfection. **For any mistakes or shortcomings, we ask Allah for His forgiveness.** May He bless this work and make it a source of guidance, inspiration, and strength for everyone who reads it.

This book seeks not only to give you knowledge but to inspire action. It aims to encourage you to read, reflect, and live by the teachings of the Quran**. May Allah guide you on your journey, and may you find His message alive in your heart.**

Faisal Sartaj

&

Aslam Sheik

Contents

Surah 1. Al-Fatihah (The Opening)

This surah is like the introduction to the Quran, a powerful prayer asking Allah for guidance. It reminds us that Allah is the Most Merciful and the true Master of Judgment Day. We ask Him to keep us on the right path, away from those who went astray.

But here's the big question: Do we really mean it when we recite it in every prayer, or are we just saying words? Imagine if Allah answered this prayer for you – are you ready to follow His guidance?

Surah 2. Al-Baqarah (The Cow)

The longest surah in the Quran is full of life lessons! It talks about faith, rules for daily life, the struggles of past nations, and the importance of patience. It warns against hypocrisy and tells us how Shaytan tricks people. It also has Ayat-ul-Kursi, the most powerful verse in the Quran!

But here's a challenge: This surah is packed with wisdom, what if you took time to read just a few verses every day and see how they connect to your life?

Surah 3. Aal-e-Imran (The Family of Imran)

This surah is named after the family of Imran (AS), which includes great figures like Maryam (Mary) (As) and Prophet Isa (Jesus) (AS). It talks about true belief, the importance of standing firm in faith, and how success comes from trusting Allah. It also tells the story of the Battle of Uhud, where a small mistake changed everything.

But here's something to think about: Do we put our full trust in Allah, or do we only turn to Him when we're in trouble?

Surah 4. An-Nisa (The Women)

This surah is all about justice—especially for women, orphans, and the weak. It teaches about fairness in marriage, inheritance, and community life. It also warns against hypocrisy and reminds us that true success comes from following Allah's guidance.

But here's a question: Islam raised the status of women over 1400 years ago – are we making sure to uphold those rights today?

Surah 5. Al-Ma'idah (The Table Spread)

This surah highlights rules for food, justice, and honesty. It tells the story of Prophet Isa's (AS) disciples asking for a heavenly feast, proof that Allah exists. But faith isn't just about seeing miracles; it's about believing even when things aren't easy. It also warns against breaking promises and changing Allah's laws.

So here's the question: If faith isn't just about miracles, what makes someone truly believe?

Surah 6. Al-An'am (The Cattle)

This surah talks about the importance of worshiping Allah alone and how people are often distracted by worldly things, like idols or desires. It shows how past nations faced consequences for rejecting the truth. It also explains how Allah's signs are everywhere if we just open our eyes.

But here's something to think about: Are we chasing after things that truly matter, or are we just caught in the rush of life?

Surah 7. Al-A'raf (The Heights)

This surah tells the story of the struggle between good and evil, focusing on prophets like Nuh (Noah)(AS), Hud (AS), and Musa (Moses) (AS). It explains how some people listen to guidance, while others reject it. It also talks about the Day of Judgment and the separation of the good from the bad.

But here's the question: Are we learning from the mistakes of past nations, or do we keep repeating them?

Surah 8. Al-Anfal (The Spoils of War)

This surah talks about the Battle of Badr, where a small group of Muslims defeated a larger enemy. It teaches us how unity, trust in Allah, and following His guidance lead to victory. It also reminds us that war should never be for personal gain, but for justice.

But here's something to think about: In our daily battles, whether personal or social, are we turning to Allah for help?

Surah 9. At-Tawbah (The Repentance)

This surah is all about sincerity and repentance. It tells us that we can always turn back to Allah, no matter how far we've strayed. It also talks about the importance of standing up for justice, even if it's hard.

But here's the big question: When was the last time we truly repented, with a sincere heart?

Surah 10. Yunus (Jonah)

The story of Prophet Yunus (AS) teaches us patience, forgiveness, and how Allah's mercy can always reach us, even from the depths of darkness. This surah emphasizes trusting Allah's plan, even when we can't see the outcome.

But here's the question: When life gets tough, do we turn to Allah first, or do we get frustrated and try to solve things on our own?

Surah 11. Hud

This surah focuses on the stories of past prophets, like Hud (AS), Nuh (AS), and Ibrahim (AS), and how they faced rejection from their people. It teaches the importance of patience, faith, and trusting Allah's plan.

But here's something to think about: If you were in the shoes of the prophets, would you stand firm in your faith, even if everyone else disagreed with you?

Surah 12. Yusuf (Joseph)

The beautiful story of Prophet Yusuf (AS) shows how patience, trust in Allah, and integrity lead to success, even when life seems unfair. This surah teaches us how jealousy, pride, and greed can destroy relationships.

But here's the question: When things don't go as planned, do we stay patient and trust that Allah has a bigger plan for us?

Surah 13. Ar-Ra'd (The Thunder)

This surah highlights Allah's supreme power over creation, using thunder as a sign of His might. It reminds us that everything in the universe follows Allah's command, yet some people still doubt Him. It speaks about the consequences of belief and disbelief, showing how faith leads to peace while denial leads to destruction. The surah assures us that Allah never breaks His promises, and those who remain patient and steadfast will be rewarded.

But here's the question: When you hear thunder, do you see it as just a sound, or as a reminder of Allah's greatness and control over everything?

Surah 14. Ibrahim (Abraham)

This surah highlights the story of Prophet Ibrahim's (AS) dedication to Allah and how he called people to worship the One true God. It teaches us that no matter how difficult life gets, the reward from Allah is worth the struggle.

But here's something to ask yourself: Do you truly trust in Allah's plan, even in the hardest times?

Surah 15. Al-Hijr (The Rocky Tract)

This surah discusses how past nations were destroyed for their arrogance and rejection of the truth. It teaches that Allah's message is clear, and we must take it seriously.

But here's the challenge: Are we paying attention to Allah's guidance, or are we distracted by the noise of the world around us?

Surah 16. An-Nahl (The Bee)

The surah reminds us of the blessings Allah gives us every day, like food, health, and even the guidance we need to live a good life. It also teaches that everything in the universe follows Allah's plan, and so should we.

But here's a question: Are we thankful for the blessings we have, or do we take them for granted?

Surah 17. Al-Isra (The Night Journey)

This surah talks about the miraculous night journey of the Prophet Muhammad ﷺ to the heavens. It emphasizes the importance of prayer, helping others, and avoiding pride. It reminds us that Allah sees everything, and there are consequences for our actions.

But here's something to think about: If you had the chance to be in the presence of Allah, would you be ready?

Surah 18. Al-Kahf (The Cave)

The surah tells the story of a group of young men who hid in a cave to escape the evil of their time. It's a reminder that faith in Allah can protect us from harm. This surah also tells other stories, like the man with two gardens, and the wise journey of Musa (AS) and Khidr (AS).

But here's the question: Are we holding onto our faith, even when the world seems against us?

Surah 19. Maryam (Mary)

This surah tells the miraculous story of Maryam (Mary) (AS), who gave birth to Isa (Jesus) (AS) despite being a virgin. It also tells us about the faith and miracles of other prophets like Zakariya (AS) and Yahya (AS). The lesson? Trust in Allah's power, no matter what.

But here's something to reflect on: If you were in Maryam's (AS) position, would you believe in miracles or doubt them?

Surah 20. Ta-Ha

This surah focuses on the story of Prophet Musa (Moses) (AS), from his early life to his mission of freeing the children of Israel. It shows how Allah helps those who trust in Him, even in the most difficult times.

But here's something to ask yourself: When facing your struggles, do you trust that Allah is there to guide you?

Surah 21.Al-Anbiya (The Prophets)

This surah tells the stories of various prophets, showing how they faced challenges, rejection, and persecution but never gave up. The message is clear: Trust in Allah's help, and don't let difficulties make you lose hope.

But here's the question: How do you react when things get tough, do you give up, or do you rely on Allah's strength?

Surah 22. Al-Hajj (The Pilgrimage)

This surah speaks about the importance of the Hajj pilgrimage and its deeper spiritual meaning. It also reminds us of the value of sacrifice and submission to Allah, as seen in the story of Prophet Ibrahim's (AS) willingness to sacrifice his son. It teaches that true strength lies in being humble before Allah.

But here's something to reflect on: Do we understand the true meaning of worship, or are we just going through the motions?

Surah 23. Al-Mu'minun (The Believers)

This surah highlights the qualities of a true believer: humility, patience, and devotion to Allah. It also emphasizes that belief isn't just about saying the right words, but living them through actions. It challenges us to examine our hearts and our intentions.

But here's the question: Do you think of yourself as a true believer? What steps can you take today to improve your faith?

Surah 24. An-Nur (The Light)

This surah emphasizes purity, modesty, and the importance of following the light of Allah's guidance. It teaches about how to live an honest life in a world full of temptations and distractions. It also warns about the consequences of immoral behavior.

But here's the challenge: Are we seeking the light of Allah in our actions, or are we blinded by the darkness of the world?

Surah 25. Al-Furqan (The Criterion)

This surah shows the distinction between truth and falsehood. It challenges us to look at our choices in life and think about whether we're following the right path. It also mentions the qualities of Allah's true servants, who act with patience and integrity.

But here's something to think about: When faced with choices, how often do you stop and think, "What would Allah want me to do?"

Surah 26. Ash-Shu'ara (The Poets)

This surah shares the stories of various prophets, like Musa (Moses)(AS) and Ibrahim (Abraham) (AS), who were rejected by their people but remained steadfast. It shows how those who stand for the truth will be challenged, but Allah's help will always come.

But here's the question: Are we ready to stand up for what's right, even when it's hard?

Surah 27. An-Naml (The Ant)

This surah highlights the wisdom and stories of various prophets, especially Prophet Sulayman (Solomon)(AS), who could speak to animals, and how Allah's signs are everywhere around us. It teaches us that true knowledge and wisdom come from trusting Allah's guidance.

But here's a thought: Do we recognize the small, hidden blessings in our lives, or do we only focus on the big ones?

Surah 28. Al-Qasas (The Stories)

This surah tells the incredible story of Prophet Musa (AS), from his birth, miraculous rescue, and life in Pharaoh's palace to his escape and rise as a prophet. It shows how Allah's plan always prevails, even when things seem hopeless. It also warns against arrogance, using the downfall of Qarun, a wealthy man who became too proud. The surah teaches us that real success lies in trusting Allah, not wealth or power.

But here's the question: If Allah could save Musa (AS) from the greatest tyrant, don't you think He can guide and protect you through your struggles too?

Surah 29. Al-Ankabut (The Spider)

This surah reminds us that faith will always be tested, just like a spider's web looks strong but is actually weak, the false beliefs people rely on will collapse in tough times. It tells stories of past nations who ignored Allah's warnings and suffered the consequences. The surah encourages believers to stay strong, trust Allah, and not be fooled by the temporary illusions of this world. True strength comes from faith, not material things.

But here's the question: When life gets tough, do you cling to fragile "spider webs," or do you rely on the unshakable support of Allah?

Surah 30. Ar-Rum (The Romans)

This surah begins with a prophecy, Allah foretells the fall and rise of the Roman Empire, proving that history unfolds by His will. It reminds us that worldly power shifts, but ultimate success belongs to believers. The surah urges us to reflect on the signs in nature, how life emerges from death, rain revives the earth, and day turns into night. These are all signs of resurrection. It warns against being distracted by worldly pleasures and forgetting the afterlife.

But here's the question: When you see history unfold, do you recognize Allah's power behind it, or do you think it's just coincidence?

Surah 31. Luqman (Luqman)

This surah shares the wise advice of Luqman, a righteous man, to his son. He teaches him to worship Allah alone, be kind to parents, pray regularly, speak with wisdom, and remain humble. It reminds us that even the smallest deeds, good or bad, will be brought to account. The surah encourages reflection on Allah's creation, the sky, mountains, and sea—all signs of His greatness. It warns against arrogance and following blind desires.

But here's something to reflect on: If you had to give one piece of advice that could change someone's life forever, what would it be?

Surah 32. As-Sajdah (The Prostration)

This surah speaks about the reality of life, death, and resurrection. It describes how some people reject the truth despite clear signs, but the true believers fall in prostration when they hear Allah's words. It reminds us of the temporary nature of this world and the ultimate justice of the Hereafter. The surah also contrasts the fate of believers and disbelievers, showing that success is not in wealth or power, but in faith and obedience.

But here's the question: When you hear the words of the Quran, do they move your heart and bring you closer to Allah?

Surah 33. Al-Azhab (The Confederates)

This surah talks about the Battle of the Confederates and how the Muslims were tested in their faith. It teaches the importance of unity and following Allah's commands, even when faced with challenges. It also mentions the Prophet's role as an example for believers.

But here's something to think about: When you face challenges, do you think about following the example of Prophet Muhammad □?

Surah 34. Saba (Sheba)

This surah highlights the rise and fall of the rich kingdom of Sheba, showing how gratitude leads to blessings while arrogance brings destruction. It contrasts the destiny of believers and disbelievers, reminding us that true success lies in obedience to Allah. The surah also speaks about the unseen, including the works of Jinn under Prophet Sulaiman (AS), proving that Allah controls everything. It warns against being deceived by wealth and power.

But here's something to think about: Are you using the blessings Allah gave you wisely, or are you letting them distract you from your purpose in life?

Surah 35. Fatir (The Originator)

This surah emphasizes Allah's infinite power as the Creator of the heavens, earth, and everything in between. It reminds us that no one can stop Allah's blessings or His punishment. The surah describes how good deeds are like pure water, giving life to the soul, while evil deeds bring only regret. It warns against being fooled by Shaytan's tricks and urges us to seek knowledge and wisdom. It also speaks about angels as powerful servants of Allah.

But here's the question: If you know that good leads to paradise and evil leads to regret, which path will you choose?

Surah 36. Ya-Sin

Known as the "heart of the Quran," this surah reminds us of Allah's power and how those who reject His message will face consequences. It also teaches us about the importance of trust in Allah and the promise of a better life for those who believe.

But here's the question: If you knew that this was your last chance to read the Quran, what would you focus on?

Surah 37. As-Saffat (The Ranks of Angels)

This surah describes the powerful and disciplined ranks of angels who obey Allah's commands without question. It tells the inspiring story of Prophet Ibrahim (AS) and his willingness to sacrifice his son for Allah's sake, proving his absolute trust in his Creator. The surah also exposes the weakness of false gods and warns about the punishment of those who mock the truth. It reassures believers that the righteous will enjoy eternal happiness in Paradise.

But here's something to reflect on: If angels, the strongest of creation, submit to Allah without hesitation, what's stopping us from fully trusting Him?

Surah 38. Sad

This surah discusses the stories of past prophets, including Dawud (David)(AS) and Sulaiman (Solomon)(AS), and the challenges they faced. It shows that no matter how powerful someone is, they are still under Allah's control. It also warns against the dangers of arrogance.

But here's something to ask yourself: Do you recognize the power of Allah in everything around you, or do you get caught up in your own abilities?

Surah 39. Az-Zumar (The Groups)

This surah talks about the consequences of following the wrong path and the rewards of following Allah's guidance. It emphasizes that on the Day of Judgment, people will be divided into two groups: the successful and the losers. It also calls people to reflect on their actions and turn to Allah for forgiveness.

But here's the challenge: If you were to be judged today, how confident would you be in your choices?

Surah 40. Ghafir (The Forgiver)

This surah reassures us that Allah's mercy is vast— He forgives sins for those who sincerely repent. It tells the story of a secret believer in Pharaoh's court who stood up for the truth despite the danger. The surah also warns about arrogance, showing how those who reject the truth will face consequences, while those who remain patient and trust Allah will be rewarded. It reminds us that every call to Allah is heard, even in tough times.

But here's the question: When you make mistakes, do you lose hope, or do you turn to Allah, the Most Forgiving?

Surah 41. Fussilat (Explained in Detail)

This surah explains in detail the signs of Allah in nature and in the Quran. It talks about how people often ignore these signs, but ultimately, they will face the truth. It also reminds us that the Quran is a clear guidance for those who are willing to listen.

But here's something to think about: Are we truly paying attention to the signs Allah has placed in our lives?

Surah 42. Ash-Shura (The Consultation)

This surah emphasizes the power of unity, humility, and seeking advice through consultation. It describes Allah's greatness in controlling the universe, sending down rain, and guiding people's hearts. The surah reminds us that true believers rely on patience, forgiveness, and trust in Allah. It also warns against arrogance and injustice, urging us to build strong communities based on justice and cooperation. The surah teaches that success isn't in power but in living with faith.

But here's something to think about: When making important decisions, do you seek wisdom and advice, or do you rely only on yourself?

Surah 43. Az-Zukhruf (The Gold Adornments)

This surah discusses how people often seek wealth and power, but those things do not bring true happiness. It tells the story of Pharaoh's arrogance and how he faced destruction. It reminds us that following the guidance of the Quran is the true way to success.

But here's a question: Are we more focused on gaining worldly riches or spiritual wealth?

Surah 44. Ad-Dukhan (The Smoke)

This surah talks about the coming punishment for those who reject the truth and the rewards for those who believe. It also warns of a great smoke that will cover the earth on the Day of Judgment. It reminds us that our actions have consequences, and only by turning to Allah can we be saved.

But here's something to reflect on: When faced with temptation, do we remember the consequences or give in?

Surah 47. Muhammad

This surah is all about the role of Prophet Muhammad ﷺ as a guide for humanity. It discusses the importance of following his example and the consequences of rejecting the truth. It also highlights the rewards for those who believe and fight in the way of Allah.

But here's a thought: How often do we truly follow the example of the Prophet □ in our lives?

Surah 48. Al-Fath (The Victory)

This surah was revealed after the Treaty of Hudaybiyyah, a key moment in the life of the Prophet ﷺ. It tells us that true victory comes from patience, faith, and submitting to Allah's will. It also highlights the importance of unity among Muslims.

But here's something to think about: Do we seek victory in the right ways, or are we chasing worldly success without considering what pleases Allah?

Surah 49. Al-Hujurat (The Rooms)

This surah teaches us the golden rules of good character; respect, kindness, and unity. It warns against gossip, backbiting, and making fun of others. It reminds us that true honor comes from piety, not wealth or status. Allah also tells us to verify information before believing or spreading it. The surah teaches that believers are one family and must resolve conflicts with wisdom. Imagine how peaceful life would be if we followed these teachings!

But here's the question: Do you judge people by their appearance, or do you look at their character, as Allah commands?

Surah 50. Qaf (The Letter Qaf)

This surah powerfully reminds us of life, death, and resurrection. It describes how Allah is closer to us than our own veins and how our every word and action is recorded. It paints a vivid picture of the Day of Judgment, when the truth will be undeniable. The surah urges us to reflect on nature; rain reviving dead land, the sky's vastness, and the mountains' stability, all signs of Allah's power.

But here's the question: If everything around you points to Allah's existence and the afterlife, what's stopping you from preparing for it?

Surah 51. Adh-Dhariyat (The Winds that Scatter)

This surah describes how the winds, clouds, and rain are all under Allah's control, reminding us of His power. It tells the story of past nations who rejected their prophets and faced destruction, warning us not to follow their path. The surah also reassures believers that their efforts in doing good are never wasted, and paradise awaits them. It reminds us that our true purpose is to worship Allah.

But here's something to think about: If Allah created you with a purpose, are you living your life in a way that fulfills it?

Surah 52. At-Tur (The Mount)

This surah starts with an oath on Mount Tur, where Allah spoke to Musa (AS). It describes the terrifying events of the Day of Judgment, where the guilty will be punished, but the righteous will enjoy endless joy in Paradise. The surah highlights the Quran's truth, challenging disbelievers who doubt it. It also comforts the Prophet ﷺ, reminding him that patience and trust in Allah lead to victory.

But here's the question: When you think about the afterlife, do you feel ready to stand before Allah, or do you feel the need to change something in your life?

Surah 53. An-Najm (The Star)

This surah confirms that the Quran is not man-made, it is divine revelation given to the Prophet ﷺ. It describes his miraculous journey of Isra and Mi'raj, where he saw the wonders of the heavens. The surah warns against blindly following false beliefs and urges people to reflect on the truth. It also reminds us that our actions determine our fate in the Hereafter. Success isn't about wealth but about righteousness.

But here's something to consider: Are you following what's right, or are you just going along with what society says is okay?

Surah 54. Al-Qamar (The Moon)

This surah begins with the astonishing miracle when the moon was split by the Prophet ﷺ, proving his truthfulness. It repeatedly warns about past nations who denied their prophets and suffered destruction. The surah stresses that the Quran is easy to understand and a reminder for those who seek guidance. It challenges those who doubt the Day of Judgment, describing its terrifying reality.

But here's something to ask yourself: When Allah constantly reminds us of past mistakes and future consequences, will you take the warning seriously or ignore it like the people before us?

Surah 55. Ar-Rahman (The Beneficent)

This surah speaks about the countless blessings of Allah, from the creation of the earth to the gifts He bestows upon humanity. It emphasizes Allah's mercy and power, urging us to be grateful and to use His gifts responsibly. It asks us to reflect on how often we thank Allah for His mercy.

But here's something to think about: How often do you truly appreciate the blessings in your life, both big and small?

Surah 56. Al-Waqi'ah (The Great Event)

This surah describes the events of the Day of Judgment and the fate of different groups of people, depending on their deeds. It emphasizes that everything in this world is temporary, and the only thing that matters is our actions. The surah encourages us to focus on earning Allah's pleasure.

But here's a thought: Are you focused on the temporary pleasures of this life, or are you preparing for the eternal success of the Hereafter?

Surah 57.Al-Hadid (The Iron)

This surah emphasizes the power of Allah, who created everything in the universe. It teaches us that true strength comes from faith in Allah and that everything we do should be in His path. It also reminds us that wealth and power are temporary, while good deeds are everlasting.

But here's the challenge: Do we use our strength and wealth to benefit others, or do we focus on self-gain?

Surah 58. Al-Mujadila (The Pleading Woman)

This surah teaches us about the importance of justice and fairness, especially in relationships. It discusses the case of a woman who pleaded to the Prophet ﷺ for help regarding an unjust situation. It reminds us that Allah hears all our pleas and that we must stand up for what's right.

But here's something to reflect on: When was the last time you stood up for someone else's rights, especially when it wasn't easy?

Surah 59. Al-Hashr (The Exile)

This surah discusses important life lessons about faith, unity, and the consequences of actions. It reminds us that everything in the universe praises Allah and that believers should trust Him. It warns against hypocrisy and encourages generosity, kindness, and supporting those in need. The surah highlights Allah's beautiful names, showing His wisdom, mercy, and power. It teaches that this world is temporary, and we should prepare for the afterlife.

But here's the big question: Are we constantly reflecting on our actions and seeking Allah's forgiveness, or are we just moving through life without thinking?

Surah 60. Al-Mumtahina (She That Is to Be examined)

This surah teaches about loyalty, trust, and kindness. It reminds believers to be cautious about whom they trust, especially when it comes to faith and enemies of Islam. However, it also encourages kindness and fairness toward those who do not fight against Muslims. The surah highlights the story of Prophet Ibrahim (AS), showing how true faith means putting Allah above all else. It also sets rules for dealing with people from different backgrounds, emphasizing justice and wisdom.

But here's something to think about: When faced with difficult relationships, do we remain firm in our faith, or do we compromise to fit in?

Surah 61. As-Saff (The Ranks)

This surah emphasizes the importance of working together in unity and standing firm in faith. It talks about the strength of the believers, and how they should be dedicated to spreading Allah's message. It also calls us to strive to be among the righteous.

But here's the question: Are we actively working to be united with others in faith, or do we let divisions distract us from our mission?

Surah 62. Al-Jumu'ah (The Friday Prayer)

This surah highlights the importance of the Friday prayer and the gathering of believers for worship. It teaches us that we should always prioritize worshiping Allah above everything else, including our work. It also emphasizes the need to learn and grow in faith.

But here's something to ask yourself: When was the last time you truly dedicated yourself to worship without distractions?

Surah 63. Al-Munafiqun (The Hypocrites)

This surah talks about the dangers of hypocrisy and how those who pretend to be believers will face severe consequences. It teaches us that sincerity in our faith is essential, and Allah sees everything.

But here's the big question: Are we being truthful in our actions and faith, or are we just pretending to be someone we're not?

Surah 64. At-Taghabun (The Mutual Disillusion)

This surah speaks about the Day of Judgment, when people will be separated into those who succeeded and those who failed. It reminds us that life's trials are a test, and that the greatest success is in the Hereafter. It also teaches us to avoid being deceived by worldly distractions.

But here's something to reflect on: Are we working toward success in this life, or are we focusing too much on what's temporary?

Surah 65. At-Talaq (The Divorce)

This surah talks about the rules of divorce and how to deal with marital issues in a respectful and just way. It emphasizes the importance of following Allah's laws in all aspects of life, even in difficult times.

But here's the question: Are we making decisions with wisdom and patience, or are we quick to act based on emotions?

Surah 66. At-Tahrim (The Prohibition)

This surah discusses the importance of protecting ourselves from actions that go against Allah's will. It talks about how the Prophet ﷺ and his family faced challenges and how they were guided to make things right. It encourages us to live with sincerity and to seek forgiveness for our mistakes.

But here's a challenge: How often do we turn to Allah in repentance, seeking to make things right when we fall short?

Surah 67. Al-Mulk (The Sovereignty)

This surah emphasizes the greatness of Allah's creation and His control over the universe. It teaches us to reflect on the signs of Allah in the world around us and remember that everything is part of His plan. The surah also reminds us of the consequences for those who reject Allah's guidance.

But here's the question: When you look at the world, do you see it as a sign of Allah's power, or do you take it for granted?

Surah 68. Al-Qalam (The Pen)

This surah highlights the importance of good character and patience, using the example of Prophet Muhammad ﷺ. It shows how those who insult or mock the truth will face consequences, while those who stand firm in their faith will be rewarded. It teaches us the value of kindness, especially when faced with criticism.

But here's something to reflect on: How do you react when people misunderstand or mock you for your beliefs?

Surah 69. Al-Haqqah (The Inevitable)

This surah paints a vivid picture of the Day of Judgment, where everything will be revealed, and the fate of every person will be sealed. It reminds us that the Hereafter is inevitable, and we should prepare for it by living righteous lives.

But here's the question: If you knew the Day of Judgment was near, what changes would you make in your life right now?

Surah 70. Al-Ma'arij (The Ascending Stairways)

This surah speaks about the journey of the soul, and how on the Day of Judgment, people will be desperate to save themselves from the consequences of their actions. It calls us to reflect on how we live our lives and the choices we make.

But here's something to think about: When you look at your life, do you see yourself heading toward success or disaster?

Surah 71. Nuh (Noah)

This surah tells the story of Prophet Nuh (AS) and his struggle to warn his people about the flood. It teaches us the importance of patience and perseverance when people ignore the truth. Despite his hard work, many people rejected him. The lesson? Stand firm in your faith, even when others don't listen.

But here's the question: If you were in Nuh's (AS) position, would you give up or keep calling people to the truth?

Surah 72. Al-Jinn (The Jinn)

This surah talks about the jinn and how they, like humans, are accountable for their actions. It reminds us that we are not alone in this world; there are unseen beings who worship Allah, just like us. It also highlights the power of the Quran to guide those who listen.

But here's something to reflect on: Do you believe that there are unseen forces at work around you, or do you only focus on what you can see?

Surah 73. Al-Muzzammil (The Enshrouded One)

This surah encourages the Prophet ﷺ, and by extension, all Muslims, to dedicate themselves to worship, especially in the night prayer (Tahajjud). It emphasizes patience, endurance, and trust in Allah when facing hardship. It reminds us that we need strength from Allah to persevere in our worship and tasks.

But here's the challenge: Do you make time for extra acts of worship, or are you too busy with the demands of the world?

Surah 74. Al-Muddathir (The Cloaked One)

This surah highlights the early stages of revelation to Prophet Muhammad ﷺ. It calls him to rise up and warn the people of the punishment that awaits those who reject the truth. It reminds us that, like the Prophet, we have a responsibility to share the message of Islam with others.

But here's something to think about: Are we sharing the message of Islam, or are we keeping it to ourselves?

Surah 75. Al-Qiyama (The Resurrection)

This surah talks about the reality of the Day of Judgment when all will be resurrected for judgment. It shows how people will be judged according to their deeds and how no one can escape Allah's justice. It encourages us to prepare for that day by living righteous lives.

But here's the question: Do you truly believe in the Day of Judgment, and does it impact how you live your life today?

Surah 76. Al-Insan (Man)

This surah discusses the creation of humans, their purpose in life, and the choices they face. It teaches us the importance of gratitude, patience, and helping others. It reminds us that this life is a test and the reward for those who live righteously is eternal.

But here's something to reflect on: Are you living with a purpose, or are you just going through the motions?

Surah 77. Al-Mursalat (The Emissaries)

This surah speaks about the angels who are sent by Allah to carry out His commands. It warns those who reject the truth and reminds them that the Day of Judgment is certain. It emphasizes that no one can escape Allah's plan.

But here's a thought: When you think about the Day of Judgment, do you feel prepared or uncertain about where you stand?

Surah 78. An-Naba (The Tidings)

This surah talks about the great news of the Day of Judgment, when everyone will see the truth. It reminds us of Allah's power to create, destroy, and resurrect, and the consequences of ignoring His signs. It challenges us to reflect on our actions and be aware of the reality of the Hereafter.

But here's the question: Do you live your life as if the Day of Judgment could come at any moment?

Surah 79. An-Nazi'at (The Soul-Snatchers)

This surah describes the angels who will take the souls of the disbelievers and the believers when the time comes. It warns of the great upheaval that will take place on the Day of Judgment and calls us to prepare for it by living a life of righteousness.

But here's something to think about: If your soul was to be taken right now, would you be ready to face Allah?

Surah 80. Abasa (He Frowned)

This surah addresses a moment in the life of Prophet Muhammad ﷺ when he turned away from a blind man who came seeking guidance. It teaches us the importance of humility and focusing on those who are truly seeking Allah's guidance. It reminds us not to judge others based on their appearance or status.

But here's the question: Do you judge others based on their outward appearance, or do you look at their hearts and intentions?

Surah 81. At-Takwir (The Overthrowing)

This surah describes the cataclysmic events of the Day of Judgment, when the sun will be folded up, the stars will fall, and everything will be turned upside down. It reminds us of the reality of the Hereafter and the consequences of our actions. It challenges us to live a life that's prepared for this inevitable event.

But here's something to think about: When you imagine the Day of Judgment, are you focused on being saved or facing regret?

Surah 82. Al-Infitar (The Cleaving)

This surah paints a vivid image of the Day of Judgment, where the sky will split open, and everyone will be held accountable for their deeds. It emphasizes that the actions we take today will determine our fate in the Hereafter. It reminds us to reflect on our choices and to seek Allah's forgiveness.

But here's a question: How much thought do you give to the consequences of your actions, knowing they will affect your eternal future?

Surah 83. Al-Mutaffifin (Defrauding)

This surah warns against cheating and dishonesty, especially in business dealings. It speaks about the people who deceive others by giving less than what is due and reminds us that Allah sees all injustice. It also warns that those who commit such acts will face consequences on the Day of Judgment.

But here's something to think about: Are we honest in our dealings, or do we sometimes cut corners for personal gain?

Surah 84. Al-Inshiqaq (The Splitting Open)

This surah discusses the splitting of the sky and the earth on the Day of Judgment, a time when everyone will be judged for their deeds. It reminds us that the truth will be evident, and we will face the results of our actions. It encourages us to strive for good deeds, as they will determine our ultimate fate.

But here's a challenge: Are you preparing for the Day of Judgment by doing good deeds every day, or are you neglecting them?

Surah 85. Al-Buruj (The Mansions of the Stars)

This surah speaks about the persecution of believers in the past, particularly the story of the young men who were martyred for their faith. It emphasizes that those who remain steadfast in their belief will be rewarded by Allah, and those who oppose the truth will face punishment.

But here's the question: Would you be willing to stand firm in your faith, even if it meant facing hardship or persecution?

Surah 86. At-Tariq (The Morning Star)

This surah describes the cosmic events that signal the end of the world, reminding us of Allah's ultimate power over creation. It emphasizes the truth of the Quran and warns against ignoring the signs of Allah. It calls us to be aware of our actions and to live in a way that prepares us for the Day of Judgment.

But here's something to reflect on: Do you recognize the signs of Allah in your life, or are you distracted by the world?

Surah 87. Al-A'la (The Most High)

This surah encourages us to praise Allah for His greatness and majesty. It speaks about the importance of remembering Allah in all aspects of life and how He is the Creator of everything in the heavens and earth. It also teaches us to purify ourselves through faith and worship.

But here's the question: How often do you take a moment to reflect on Allah's greatness in your everyday life?

Surah 88. Al-Ghashiyah (The Overwhelming)

This surah describes the overwhelming events of the Day of Judgment when some people will be in a state of bliss and others will be in suffering. It reminds us of the consequences of our actions and urges us to choose the right path.

But here's something to think about: When you think about the Day of Judgment, do you focus on preparing for paradise or avoiding punishment?

Surah 89. Al-Fajr (The Dawn)

This surah emphasizes the importance of reflection and gratitude. It talks about the destruction of past nations who were arrogant and rejected Allah's message. It encourages us to learn from their mistakes and strive for righteousness.

But here's the challenge: When you face difficulty, do you reflect on the blessings of Allah or fall into despair?

Surah 90. Al-Balad (The City)

This surah reminds us of the blessings of life in a city and the responsibilities that come with them. It calls us to reflect on the choices we make, whether we live for this world alone or choose to work for the Hereafter. It teaches us that Allah's guidance leads us to success.

But here's something to think about: Are you making choices today that will lead to success in the Hereafter?

Surah 91. Ash-Shams (The Sun)

This surah emphasizes the importance of self-purification and being true to our inner selves. It talks about how the soul has been created with both potential for good and evil, and it is up to us to choose which path we take. The surah calls us to purify our hearts and follow the right path.

But here's the question: Do you focus on purifying your heart, or are you distracted by the world's desires?

Surah 92. Al-Lail (The Night)

This surah contrasts the paths of those who choose good and those who choose evil. It teaches us that our choices have consequences, and the path of righteousness leads to ultimate success. It also emphasizes the importance of charity and helping others.

But here's something to reflect on: Are you making decisions based on what will help you in the Hereafter, or are you focused on temporary rewards?

Surah 93. Ad-Duha (The Morning)

This surah reassures the Prophet ﷺ, telling him that after hardship comes ease, and that Allah has not forsaken him. It encourages gratitude for Allah's blessings and reminds us that Allah's mercy is always with those who are patient. The surah calls us to remember Allah in times of difficulty and to give to those in need.

But here's something to reflect on: When life gets tough, do you lose hope, or do you trust that Allah's mercy will guide you through?

Surah 94. Al-Inshirah (The Relief)

This surah is a message of hope! It reminds us that after every hardship comes ease. Allah reassures the Prophet ﷺ, and all of us, that struggles are temporary, and relief is always near. Life can feel overwhelming, but this surah teaches us to stay patient and keep striving. Allah has lifted burdens before and will do so again. The key is to keep turning to Him and never give up.

But here's the question: When life gets tough, do you lose hope, or do you trust that Allah is preparing you for something better?

Surah 95. At-Tin (The Fig)

This surah highlights the honor of human creation, Allah made us in the best form! But those who turn away from faith lower themselves, while those who do good will have a great reward. Allah swears by the fig and olive, reminding us of the lands of revelation, where great prophets were sent. This surah makes us reflect on our actions, are we living up to our purpose? Are we valuing the blessings Allah gave us?

But here's something to think about: If Allah created you in the best way, are you making choices that reflect your true potential?

Surah 96. Al-Alaq (The Clot)

This surah begins with the command to "Read" in the name of Allah, highlighting the importance of knowledge and seeking understanding. It speaks about the creation of humanity and the role of knowledge in our lives. The surah emphasizes that everything we do should be for the sake of Allah.

But here's the question: How much value do you place on seeking knowledge, and how does that knowledge influence your faith and actions?

Surah 97. Al-Qadr (The Power)

This surah describes the greatness of Laylat al-Qadr, the Night of Decree, when the Quran was revealed. It emphasizes that this night is better than a thousand months, and encourages us to seek Allah's mercy and forgiveness during this blessed time. The surah highlights the importance of prayer, supplication, and striving to make the most of our opportunities.

But here's a thought: How do you plan to make the most of Laylat al-Qadr, and what steps will you take to increase your worship during Ramadan?

Surah 98. Al-Bayyina (The Clear Proof)

This surah speaks about the clear proof of the truth of Islam, revealed through the Prophet Muhammad ﷺ and the Quran. It emphasizes the importance of accepting the truth and following it, while warning those who reject it. The surah calls us to live according to the clear guidance of Islam and to be a positive example for others.

But here's something to think about: Do you follow the clear guidance of Islam in your life, or do you let doubts and distractions lead you away from the truth?

Surah 99. Az-Zalzalah (The Earthquake)

This surah describes the mighty earthquake that will occur on the Day of Judgment, when the earth will reveal everything it has contained. It reminds us that on that day, everyone will be judged for their actions, and their deeds will be displayed before them. The surah calls us to reflect on the consequences of our choices and to be aware that everything we do matters.

But here's the question: Are you conscious of the fact that every action you take will be revealed on the Day of Judgment?

Surah 100. Al-Adiyat (The Courser)

This surah speaks about the horses that gallop in battle, emphasizing the speed and power of their charge. It compares the disbelievers' greed and ignorance to the rushing of these horses. The surah calls us to be aware of our selfish desires and to use our strength and energy in the service of Allah. It reminds us that we are accountable for our actions.

But here's something to reflect on: Are you using your energy for good, or are you driven by desires that lead you away from Allah?

Surah 101. Al-Qari'ah (The Striking Calamity)

This surah speaks about the striking calamity that will occur on the Day of Judgment, a time of intense fear and upheaval. It describes how people will be judged based on their deeds, and the weight of good actions will determine their fate. The surah challenges us to reflect on the importance of doing righteous deeds.

But here's the question: Do you live in a way that ensures your deeds will be heavy on the scales of good on the Day of Judgment?

<u>Surah 102. At-Takathur (The Rivalry in Worldly Increase)</u>

This surah warns against the rivalry and obsession with accumulating wealth and material possessions. It reminds us that in the end, these things will not matter, and we will be held accountable for how we spent our time. The surah calls us to focus on what truly matters: good deeds and devotion to Allah.

But here's something to think about: Are you more focused on collecting material wealth, or on collecting good deeds for the Hereafter?

Surah 103. Al-Asr (The Time)

This surah emphasizes the importance of time and the value of using it wisely. It reminds us that all of humanity is in a state of loss, except those who believe, do good deeds, and encourage others to do the same. The surah highlights the significance of living with purpose and striving to do good in our limited time.

But here's a thought: How are you spending your time? Are you using it to benefit your faith, or are you wasting it on things that won't matter in the end?

Surah 104. Al-Humazah (The Slanderer)

This surah warns against backbiting, slandering, and mocking others. It emphasizes that those who engage in such behaviors will face severe consequences on the Day of Judgment. The surah calls us to be mindful of our words and actions, and to treat others with respect and kindness.

But here's something to reflect on: How often do you speak about others behind their backs, and how do your words reflect your character?

Surah 105. Al-Fil (The Elephant)

This surah tells the story of the army of the elephant, led by Abraha, who intended to destroy the Ka'bah but was defeated by the power of Allah. The surah highlights Allah's ability to protect His house and His people. It reminds us that no one can oppose Allah's will.

But here's the question: When you face challenges, do you rely on your strength or do you trust in Allah's power to help you overcome them?

Surah 106. Quraysh (The Quraysh)

This surah speaks about the blessings Allah granted to the tribe of Quraysh, especially their safety during trade journeys. It encourages gratitude for Allah's protection and provisions. The surah calls us to be thankful for the blessings we often take for granted.

But here's something to think about: Do you express gratitude to Allah for the countless blessings in your life, or do you overlook them in your daily routine?

Surah 107. Al-Ma'un (The Small Kindnesses)

This surah emphasizes the importance of helping others and showing kindness. It criticizes those who neglect the needy and the orphan, and those who perform acts of worship only for show. The surah calls us to be sincere in our faith and to act with compassion.

But here's the question: Do you help those in need, or do you focus only on your own well-being and ignore the needs of others?

Surah 108. Al-Kawthar (The Abundance)

This surah speaks about the great blessings and rewards that Allah has granted to the Prophet Muhammad ﷺ, particularly the river of Al-Kawthar in Paradise. It encourages us to be thankful for Allah's abundant blessings and to perform acts of worship sincerely. The surah calls us to pray and make sacrifices for Allah.

But here's a thought: How do you show your gratitude to Allah for His countless blessings in your life?

Surah 109. Al-Kafirun (The Disbelievers)

This surah is a clear declaration of the distinction between the believers and the disbelievers. It emphasizes that there is no compromise in matters of faith, Muslims worship Allah alone and will not associate any partners with Him. The surah encourages us to stay firm in our faith and not to be influenced by the beliefs of others.

But here's the question: Are you confident in your belief in Allah, or do you sometimes feel pressured to compromise your faith?

Surah 110. An-Nasr (The Divine Support)

This surah speaks about the victory granted to the Prophet Muhammad ﷺ and his followers. It celebrates the conquest of Makkah and the triumph of Islam. It also reminds us that with victory comes the responsibility to thank Allah and seek His forgiveness. The surah calls us to praise Allah and turn to Him in gratitude.

But here's something to reflect on: When you experience success in life, do you remember to thank Allah, or do you take credit for it yourself?

Surah 111. Al-Masad (The Palm Fiber)

This surah condemns the wife of Abu Lahab and her role in opposing the Prophet ﷺ. It warns against arrogance, pride, and those who work against Allah's message. The surah also serves as a reminder that no one can escape the consequences of their actions.

But here's the question: Do you align yourself with righteousness, or do you follow the negative influences around you, despite knowing the consequences?

Surah 112. Al-Ikhlas (The Purity)

This surah is a declaration of the absolute oneness and uniqueness of Allah. It emphasizes that Allah is beyond compare, and that He is not in need of anyone or anything. The surah reminds us that the foundation of faith is acknowledging the true nature of Allah.

But here's something to think about: Do you fully understand and believe in the oneness of Allah, or do you sometimes struggle to grasp His greatness?

Surah 113. Al-Falaq (The Daybreak)

This surah seeks protection from the evil forces in the world, including envy, darkness, and harmful creatures. It reminds us that Allah is the ultimate source of protection and refuge. The surah encourages us to seek refuge in Allah from all forms of harm and to trust in His power.

But here's the question: When faced with challenges, do you turn to Allah for protection, or do you rely on your own strength?

Surah 114. An-Nas (The People)

This surah is a prayer for protection from the whispers of evil, both from humans and jinn. It emphasizes the importance of seeking refuge in Allah from harm and evil. The surah calls us to stay close to Allah and to ask for His help in every aspect of our lives.

But here's something to reflect on: How often do you turn to Allah for help when facing difficulties, and how often do you try to handle things on your own?

"Indeed, this Quran guides to that which is most suitable."

– Surah Al-Isra (17:9)